C.S.S. Publishing Co., Inc.

Lima, Ohio

CATERPILLARS, COCOONS, AND BUTTERFLIES

8823 / ISBN 1-55673-052-7   PRINTED IN U.S.A.

Table of Contents

Easter   5

   Easter Sunrise Service   6

   Easter Festival Service   8

   An Easter Meditation
      Caterpillars, Cocoons, and Butterflies   12

Easter

Easter Sunday ranks second only to Christmas as *the* great festival of the Christian church year. It is the day on which Jesus rose from the dead. It is also referred to as Resurrection Sunday. It was observed as early as the second century A.D. It sets apart Sunday, the first day of the week, as the Christian day of worship for most denominations.

Today, Easter is observed on the first Sunday following the first full moon after the spring equinox. Thus it is a movable date, unlike Christmas. That date was set by the Council of Nicaea in A.D. 325. The feast of the Resurrection coincided with the pagan rites of spring. The word Easter comes from the name of the (dawn) goddess, *Eastre*. The earth, with its renewal after the cold and seeming death of winter in the northern hemisphere, powerfully reinforces the great truth Easter declares: the triumph of life over death, light over darkness, faith over doubt and fear. Through Christ, we, too, can be renewed from the dark binding of sin to the freedom of light and eternal life.

Easter Sunrise Service

(*Congregation stand)

PRELUDE

OPENING PRAYER   O God, who makes the stars, and turns the shadow of death into the morning: on this day of days we meet to render you, our Lord and King, the tribute of our praise; for the resurrection of springtime, for the everlasting hopes that rise within the human heart, and for the Gospel which has brought life and immortality to light. Receive our thanksgiving, reveal your presence, and send into our hearts the Spirit of the risen Christ. Amen

*HYMN   *"Were You There?"*

    READER #1   ***The Testimony of the Women***
           Luke 23:55-56; 24:1-6, 9-11

    FAMILY CHOIR *"My Lord, What a Morning"*

    READER #2   ***Jesus on the Emmaus Road***
           Luke 24:13-21, 25-31, 33-35

HYMN   *"Low in the Grave He Lay"*[or another suitable hymn]
[Start out softly, build to climax]

    READER #3   ***Jesus Appears to the Ten in the Upper Room***
           John 20:19-23

    READER #4   ***Jesus Appears to Doubting Thomas***
           John 20:24-31

    FAMILY CHOIR *"What Wondrous Love Is This?"*

READER #2 *Jesus Appears to the Eleven on a Mountain in Galilee*
Matthew 28:16-20; Mark 16:19-20

READER #1 There were many others who witnessed his resurrection: Nicodemus, Joseph of Arimathea, all the disciples except Judas. He appeared to as many as five hundred at one time. Let us hear the testimony from St. Paul in 1 Corinthians 15:3-24. [*Read*] The living Christ is real. He gave new life to us. He gives new life to all who believe, trust him, have faith in him.

***CLOSING HYMN** *"Christ the Lord Is Risen Today"*

***BENEDICTION**

POSTLUDE

Easter Festival Service

*(*Congregation stand)*

PRELUDE

TRUMPET FANFARE

***CALL TO WORSHIP**
Make a joyful noise to the Lord, all the earth; break forth into joyous song and sing praises! Sing praises to the Lord with the lyre, with the lyre and the sound of melody! With trumpet and the sound of the horn make a joyful noise before the King, the Lord!

(Psalm 98:4-6)

***PROCESSIONAL HYMN**
"Thine Is the Glory"
[Parade of banners, balloons, and butterflies]

ADORATION OF THE RISEN LORD

Pastor:	Now on the first day of the week Mary Magdalene came to the tomb early, while it was still dark, and saw that the stone had been taken away from the tomb. (John 20:1)
People:	**Hallelujah, the Lord is risen!**
Pastor:	So they [the women] departed quickly from the tomb with fear and great joy, and ran to tell his disciples. And behold, Jesus met them and said, "Hail!" And they came up and took hold of his feet and worshiped him. (Matthew 28:8,9)
People:	**Hallelujah, the Lord is risen!**

Pastor: But Mary stood weeping outside the tomb, and as she wept she stooped to look into the tomb; and she saw two angels in white, sitting where the body of Jesus had lain, one at the head and one at the feet. They said to her, "Woman, why are you weeping?" She said to them, "Because they have taken away my Lord, and I do not know where they have laid him." Saying this, she turned round and saw Jesus standing, but she did not know that it was Jesus. Jesus said to her, "Woman, why are you weeping? Whom do you seek?" Supposing him to be the gardener, she said to him, "Sir, if you have carried him away, tell me where you have laid him, and I will take him away." Jesus said to her, "Mary." She turned and said to him in Hebrew, "Rabboni!" (which means Teacher).

(John 20:11-16)

People: Hallelujah, Christ is risen!

Pastor: That very day two of them were going to a village named Emmaus, about seven miles from Jerusalem, and talking with each other about all these things that had happened. While they were talking and discussing together, Jesus himself drew near and went with them.

(Luke 24:13-15)

People: Hallelujah, Christ is risen!

10

Pastor: On the evening of that day, the first day of the week, the doors being shut where the disciples were, for fear of the Jews, Jesus came and stood among them and said to them, "Peace be with you." When he had said this, he showed them his hands and his side. Then the disciples were glad when they saw the Lord.   (John 20:19-20)

People: **Hallelujah, Jesus the Christ is risen!**

Pastor: Simon Peter said to them, "I am going fishing." They said to him, "We will go with you." They went out and got into the boat; but that night they caught nothing. Just as day was breaking, Jesus stood on the beach; yet the disciples did not know that it was Jesus. That disciple whom Jesus loved said to Peter, "It is the Lord!"   (John 21:3-4, 7a)

People: **Hallelujah, our Lord is risen!**

Pastor: I was in the Spirit on the Lord's day, and heard behind me a great voice as of a trumpet. And I turned to see the voice that was speaking to me. Being turned, I saw one like a son of man, clothed with a long robe and with a golden girdle round his breast; his head and his hair were white as snow; his feet like burnished bronze, and his voice like the sound of many waters. When I saw him, I fell at

his feet as though dead. But he laid his right hand upon me, saying, "Fear not. I am the first and the last, and the living one; I died, and behold I am alive for evermore, and I have the keys of hell and death.
(Revelation 1:10, 12-18, paraphrased)

People: **Hallelujah! Hallelujah! Hallelujah!**

ANTHEM

PASTORAL PRAYER

LORD'S PRAYER

OFFERTORY ANTHEM

***DOXOLOGY AND DEDICATION OF GIFTS**

***HYMN** *"All Hail the Power of Jesus' Name"*

SCRIPTURE **1 Corinthians 1:18-31**

SERMON *Caterpillars, Cocoons and Butterflies*

***RECESSIONAL HYMN** *"I Serve a Risen Savior"*
[or another appropriate hymn]

***BENEDICTION**

POSTLUDE

12

An Easter Meditation

Caterpillars, Cocoons, and Butterflies

1 Corinthians 1:18-31

First, let me share with you another Scripture, John 3:1-7, from the Barclay translation:

> *There was a man who was one of the Pharisees who was called Nicodemus, a ruler of the Jews. He came to Jesus by night and said to Him: "Rabbi, we know that you are a teacher who has come from God, for no one can do the signs which you do unless God is with him." Jesus answered him: "This is the truth I tell you — unless a man is reborn from above, he cannot see the Kingdom of God." Nicodemus said to Him: "How can a man be born when he is old? Surely he cannot enter into his mother's womb a second time and be born?" Jesus answered: "This is the truth, I tell you — unless a man is born of water and the Spirit he cannot enter into the Kingdom of God. That which is born from the flesh is flesh, and that which is born of the Spirit is spirit."*

Is it possible for a person to be reborn? What seems foolish or impossible to us is possible in God's wisdom. We don't always understand. "What looks like God's foolishness is wiser than men's wisdom; and what looks like God's weakness is stronger than men's strength." (1 Corinthians 1:25)

In the book of Job we find Job lamenting his birth and the way God runs the universe. The Lord answers Job out of a whirlwind:

> *"Where were you when I laid the foundation of the earth? Tell me, if you have understanding." (38:4)*

"Will the faultfinder contend with the Almighty? Let him who reproves God answer it."

Then Job answered the Lord and said, "Behold, I am insignificant; what can I reply to Thee? I lay my hand on my mouth. Once I have spoken, and I will not answer. Even twice, and I will add no more." (40:2-5 NAS)

We, too, are to stand in awe of God's wisdom and learn from it. To the question of Nicodemus', "How can a man be born when he is old? Surely he cannot enter into his mother's womb a second time and be born," we would turn our minds to the lesson God teaches us in caterpillars, cocoons, and butterflies.

1. Caterpillars

Caterpillars come in all sizes and shapes and colors — brown ones, green ones, fat ones, skinny ones, spotted ones, some beautiful, some ugly, some smooth skin, some furry. Sounds a lot like people, doesn't it?

Isaac Watts, the great hymn writer, wrote the song, "Alas, And Did My Savior Bleed?" In the original first stanza he wrote:

Alas! And did my Savior bleed?
And did my sovereign die?
Would he devote that sacred head
For such a worm as I?

Over the years, people objected to being called a worm. In some hymnals that last line is changed to, "For sinners such as I?" I really don't understand the difference between sinner and worm.

Ernest Emurian, author and United Methodist pastor, plus a leader of hymn festivals, writes:

"I wrote my own rebuttal in a four-line poem that contains these lines: It used to seem absurd to me, to sing of 'such a worm as I', Until I saw an ugly worm, become a gorgeous butterfly!"

I heartily agree. Possibly Watt's figures of speech were actually closer to the heart of the Gospel than those alterations of his critics. The change wrought in the human heart, whereby a sinner dies that a saint may be born, has its parallel in nature, when a worm dies that a butterfly may be born!

Paul says in Romans 12:2 (NAS), "And do not be conformed to this world, but be transformed by the renewing of your mind, that you may prove what the will of God is, that which is good and acceptable and perfect."

2. Cocoons

The cocoon is the resting form in which the worm or larvae transform into adults. Most butterflies and moths spend the winter as pupae. Each kind of caterpillar spins, in its own way, a cocoon that surrounds itself. Through the long winter months, the cocoon hangs from a twig like a dead leaf.

But what is inside is dying to itself, in order that it might begin something new. It will never be the same as when it went in.

Nicodemus asked of Jesus if a man must enter back into his mother's womb to be born again. The cocoon is like a womb. It protects while changes are being made. If the caterpillar obeys the commands of its nature, thereby God's plan, something marvelous will happen. When the process is over, the butterfly will emerge, with marked changes in character, form, and appearance.

But most of us human beings resist change. We do not want to go through the process of metamorphosis. We do not want transformation. We would rather conform to the ways of the world.

We say, "I'm not going to change for anybody." Or we say, "Why should I change? I'm young; I've got my whole life before me. I've got to do it my way." Or, "I'm too old to change, too set in my ways."

We don't want anyone interfering with our life. Consequently, old habits do not change; old attitudes do not change; old behavior patterns do not change. We lumber along the same old rut to our grave. What Jesus opens up for us is the possibility of entering into a spiritual cocoon that we may emerge a new creation. St. Paul tells us: "Therefore, if any one is in Christ, he is a new creation; the old has passed away, behold, the new has come. All this is from God, who through Christ has reconciled us to himself and gave to us the ministry of reconciliation; that is, God was in Christ reconciling the world to himself, not counting their trespasses against them, and entrusting to us the message of reconciliation." (2 Corinthians 5:17-19)

Through God's act of sacrifice of Jesus Christ on the cross, the process of being a forgiven human being is forever sealed. When we come to God through the loving and forgiving act of the cross, we enter the spiritual cocoon by which we may be changed. Like a cocoon hanging on a dead limb in the midst of winter, we shall be changed.

3. Butterflies

You and I do not understand all the process of going from caterpillar to butterfly. But we see the results. Jesus says to Nicodemus, "The wind blows where it wills, and you hear the sound of it, but you do not know whence it comes or whither it goes; so it is with every one who is born of the Spirit." (John 3:8) We do see the results; we feel them; we can testify to them.

Like the caterpillar, we must give up our *caterpillar-ness*. We must die to our selfishness, our sin, our hate, our prejudice. We must cooperate with the nature of God's will for our lives.

We must allow the cocoon of God's love to surround us. If we allow Jesus to be the catalyst, he will transform us. He is the one who makes us new. He is with us in the winter of our sorrow for sin and repentance. It is through his patient love and forgiveness that we are freed from those things that bind us to sin. We must put on the cocoon of Jesus, rather than the cocoon of sin.

The promise of God is that we shall be changed. We shall be changed into the beautiful creatures that God has always meant us to be. He did not intend that we be stained with sin. We were not meant to crawl all our lives. We were meant to fly!

Conclusion

We are made in the image of God. That image is like a beautiful butterfly. But mankind as a whole and individually, by their decision to sin, has marred that image. We became like worms. We don't have to remain that way. There is a way through Jesus Christ. Therefore, be butterflies.